... Emptied of All Ships

Some of these poems have appeared in *Drill, Xcp: Cross Cultural Poetics, The Cultural Society, Antennae, 26, Dodo Bird & Court Green*. "Some Mariners" was published as a chapbook by EtherDome Press. "Emptied of All Ships" was published as a chapbook by Bronze Skull Press. The poem beginning "mummified arm" in "Some Mariners" was printed as a broadside by Cuneiform Press.

Thank you to the editors, readings series coordinators and friends who have supported me throughout the writing of these poems. This book is dedicated to my poet comrades in Milwaukee, Madison and Chicago.

ISBN: 0-923331-6-9

Cover art: Brenda Iijima
Cover design: Brenda Iijima & E. Tracy Grinnell
Typesetting & book design: E. Tracy Grinnell
Drawings: Drew Kunz

Distributed by Small Press Distribution
1341 Seventh St. Berkeley, CA 94170
www.spdbooks.org

Emptied
of
All Ships

...

Stacy Szymaszek

LITMUS PRESS

BROOKLYN • 2005

Contents

... shift at oars

water
relives
reservoir

boat
bottom
draft
displaced

o

lineal
thought
backward
body

no one
knows
the brains
I am now

tree
an oar
origin

joints ruptured
soak in
deep ink

o

wallpaper
remnant
flower
float

chandelier

brief case
hundred words
logged

erode
my
Arabic

congestion
of resin

person

forecasts
final position

restless sleep

o

width of
back
belted

sodium
poultice

exhausts
courtship

agora

drain
a home
of you

wind
lashes
fronds

cellophane

o

where a
mammal
bled

activity
not yet
diffused

blackened
patch
of water

weight
of oyster
in gloved
hand he
shucks

dented
pewter

      o

assonance
her aspect

relocated

wind
shatters
plexi

phenomena
foregone
for me

shift
at oars

new
muscle
grown
bone

never
held
you

o

case
of dried
apricot

gorge

I am
summoned

capable
a day

outlast
forecast

coral reef

feeler

o

paper
cover
mallet
awl

downfall

fire-
box

androgyne

... ballast

ceramic
Jesus
medallion
with chipped
features

contents
of a secret-
bottomed
drawer
yellowed
song
lyrics
wax
phallus
mending
kit

Latin
dictionary
German
crossword
series
of curtailed
letters

my embroidered
misnomer

pouch
of dead
teeth
everything
from
China

guide
by a Polish
sailor
gold-plated
cabinet
handles
radio
apparatus

... auction

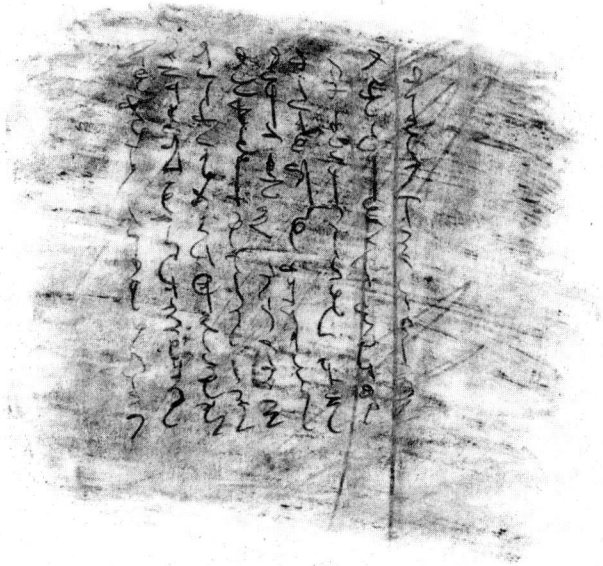

one sketch
of the stormy
petrel

one set of clothes
not to be worn
during the voyage

one log
of the harm
that came

you
miss
a man
so much

music
for Haul
On the
Bowline

slop
chest

small
stuff

prayer
book

Green-
lander
with
a stitch
through
his nose

coin in
his mouth

his custody

broken
holy
stone
at feet
sailmaker
stitches you
inside a sail

last to
touch

your craft

slipped
starboard

pig
on
foot
does
no
good

to stay afloat
to assure
identity

one pot
of ink

one paragraph
on a miscellaneous
custom

quit
the
American
shore
quit
the
shore
of Green-
land

miss
a man

pot of
wood ash

box
of blank
cards

beef bone
sculpture

deducted
from
wages
what
you
bid

seldom
mentioned
in leisure

his form
forecastle
slip

cliché
poor guy…

the oath
and the laugh
boom

skylark
flicks a card
in another's
face

… radio silence

I puff
words
into
a brass
speaking
tube

to preserve
radio silence

what seems
a cipher to
the populace

a broadcast
to one ear

lucid as
the bulletins
it could prove
fraudulent
in time

two chambers
are connected
here

I hammer
an ashtray
out of
copper

ting—ting-ting—tong

an afternoon
to say
"I hurt
my knee"

never mind
I need a salve

I leave
a tin of sardines
open for
a month

is it
still
you
there?

binding
the pages
with lead
plates
and
throwing
them
overboard

... sailor king

quartered
with a pipe
ignores
the fracas

friends
in boyhood
joggle him

special
one who
taught him
to smoke

      o

floating castle
peace time
waters

while
Normandy
rages

he lengthens
his accordian

thinks of
his guns
in *Daar Sanaa*

he is thought
to possess

a charm

his friends
walk past
his house
in leathers
motioning

that renders him
lawless

o

every sea
a battle scene
cast anchor
and survey
promptness
of sharks

o

aerate pipe
stride the
deck
his image
recurs in
vignettes

now back to
the fracas

a petition
is signed
in a pattern
spokes of
a wheel
grievance at
the pilot

who keeps
looking back
to shore

o

holograph
of his kin
wife's hands
waving

horizon
of surplus
hats

tilt
image

hats fly
through
the air

o

the round
robin chants
make-them-stop-calling

sailor king
orders up
a shantyman

"sing
the man
to sleep"

... manifest

defunct
list of
common
names
proxy
for the
bearer

nor'wester
buffets gear
reach
into our
canisters

"Cassirer"
drawn and
sewn into
my lapels
assembly of
illegal men
peril will
not know

two
Roman
slaves
gulp rain
the rage
passes
through our
teeth into
interior
pneumatic
doors

my evening
of moniker
stamped
upon boxes
of envelopes

blank
ledger
for you
"Macquin"
with tin
and amber
stockpiled
you prince

... emptied of all ships

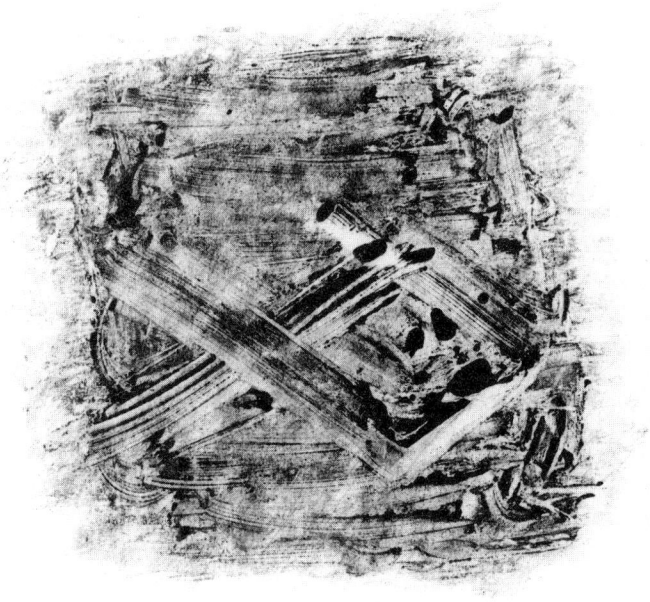

I

ships launch
into world
from stripe
in garb
chemical sails
float them far

ships launch
into world
from crash
in flesh
tugboats
tow them far

ships launch
into world
from excised
anchor
reef knots
pull them far

watch blips
on hour

hand glides
into chest
of slippery
combs

emptied of
all ships

II

mother
folds
sails
as I
count
flower
parts

inside
parrot
feather
fossil
against
aorta

sip of
soda

Pompeii

ash in
orange
wedge

hummingbird
maw

III

jettison
winged lung

red print
thumb

hot
Egyptian
cotton

sinus

Elysium

IV

shed on
property

clamp
light

peripheral

know
where
it is

Cypress
radio

V

swordfish
unravels spool
of filament

sleek
headed

swim it

East

fisherman
pseudonym

Finnish
has the
flashlight

VI

game of
checkers

wood-
pecker

gazebo
lemon

marlin

wide
brim

song
belted
in a note
thought
mutineer

VII

unfurl
or fold

Chinese
screen

cloak
my figure
within
its landscape

great
gold-
fish

VIII

cherry
cig
poker
chips

isl.

where
I sent him

bell-bottomed
I won
wrong
woman
called

streamers
in my face

IX

perspire

an August
tempest

then
shutter
pores

X

Nefertiti

Arabic folder

14 c.

jackel
and me

drape
costume
a tent
for two

which
pitched

swathed
in cabinet

letter

frigate

... figurehead

glass
eyes
fixed
into
wood
flanks

beak
juts
tale
wakes

sentient
as I

you
turned
away
fast

with
your
banner

GOODBYE!

... some mariners

sequent of waves albumen ferment
white cap floats hum syllables of elegy

veer anchor train to sea bottom—pendulums
Darwins of sound gull song obscure

in wide air—tintinnabular—sympathetic
under tonnage of flora ocean of phantom brain

grieve with me—Slavic   Indic   Arabic

James caresses

a silver fish

his eyes sunspots

against sunrise

envisions his tan arm

in a Sicilian net

gilled and thrashing

pulled by

tides so vast

they are invisible

Corsair speeds

above ancient stands

with atomic

clocks in her gut

procures a month

of daylight

midnight yelling

we see a blue arm

in the offing

firmament tears open

baring what was

our access

piratical skuas

laying claim to our islet

beat their broad wings

hold us in orbit

my injury cool

with atomized liquid

set unstable table

make myslf attractive

quill in my pocket

drink ink from China

James's feeling arm

is full — I'm

SWALLOWS WITH BANNERS

the sail menders with hands

and feet repair into dawn

trailing bolts of canvas

maneuver fish needles in half light

reach top velocity in

pantheistic celebration

let us not forget the restraints of

our vessel when in ash you enter

invertebrate sea

funnel into whalebone

form your love will seek

every plasm remembered

through my constant dream

beneath the tarpaulin

you are a sea monster

I am your sea

```
          p                   o
  r       l                   u
    u       u       f           t
    b       m       r           e           s
    i       m           o           r           p
    e       e               m                   a
      s       t                                     c
                                                    e
```

black clouds. spilled ink

progression of centuries. drunk at night watch tower

wrote five letters

black clouds. spilled ink blotting out Balkan peninsula

pale rain. beads spatter the tarpaulin

police force wind comes. blasts and scatters them

true solar year is more than a year. pesky fraction

below night watch tower. ocean like sky

after Su Tung-P'o
translated by James

spirited tars brawl sunward

one holds a reptile egg

who is too pretty to smack

holds the egg to the sun's

thermal bottom

alias James

arm
an alloy

ambidextrous
wonder

yd never

touch

bodies of fishes swell

from white hot sea

Krakatoan explosion!

rim pharos alerted by

wave stressed ambits

reclaim one adrift on a fin

laden sun metallurgic

in a closet

full of melons

we are slats

of a dining table

whorling together

in gradual slope

hatch the surface

with your teeth

then meet me

in the evening

underneath

ink a hinge here

'n here

'n mother

make me limber

grappling iron your legs

moor me in full tide

whet against protean shoulders

breath is fuel open your mouth

seep into luminous prowl of sea

night is shell eloquent

transient lid

on a ship. awake at night

cool wind bends your trim hazel hair

I open the hatch. pink moon pulls. a colossal bobbin

boat men and sea birds dream the same dream

dorsal fin splashes. baleen hinge creaks beneath

it's late. creatures and people forget each other

I'd like to amuse you. clever with anchors and cables

time passes swiftly when you eat   sleep   fuck

whenever you want. I use my sorrow

a scene like this? it can't last long

after Su Tung-P'o
translated by James

private room

James dresses

black flannel

water glows

alphabets flicker

circular windows

transmits a letter

i   t   h   i   n   k
          o   f   y   o   u
               o   f   t   e   n

into the mind of his lover

July corridor

Affined rim

Mum   *mum*   when

Echoic   I descry further

Species

easy in sleep

you nuzzle me

betraying your

tortured belly

the skin begins

coda of whales

the fragrance of you

the body that permits itself a dream
is drunk on plum wine by dusk

after Yu Xuanji
translated by James

trail of clothes

life uncorded

my sweat glows

knock the hat off

swill my brain

ship followers song reports

within watch coats

inner pockets of stale cake

will joint voyage for

bodily eruption from plaits

downy mast head meeting

meteor de-orbits

and burns

re-enters what was Friday

20 tons

of debris

O people on Fiiijiii!

divide hour into smaller units

water clock futurist

mind leaks grass whistles

field of peacock blue

||||| ||||| ||||| ||||| ||||| ||||| |||||

||||| ||||| ||||| ||||| ||||| ||||| |||||

||||| ||||| ||||| ||||| ||||| ||||| |||||

||||| ||||| ||||| ||||| ||||| ||||| |||||

||||| ||||| ||||| ||||| ||||| ||||| |||||

||||| ||||| ||||| ||||| ||||| ||||| |||||

||||| ||||| ||||| ||||| ||||| ||||| |||||

ORA   PASSIM

how can I sleep through a night with no end?

I get up and scrawl   lines of words   I wish   I didn't exist

as lightning destroys the sky   and the sea wants the boat

I open my night shirt   let the torrent

drum my body   my shell hardened breast   my unbattened
sex

all the people in the world   and I can only think of you   in the
curvature of rain

all the wrecks it has seen   a bird circles exhaling darkness

after Yuan Chi and Anonymous (Six Dynasties)
translated by James

78

dream

a thousand sails wait in the nimbus. merge with injured fish

blue sun towed beneath the horizon. I am rapt

in your maw and feel you asking. *where are you going?*

my oratory is a gurgle of scales and water. evolved birds

fly the diameter of wind. moons rip out

forming new sea bottoms. O tides don't stop

till I am catapulted into the center of the Eastern Sea

after li Ch'ing-chao
translated by James

chest of phalli cradle

hands to torso till rose

hips in bowl crushed

dark pit of mollusk

lip down scoliatic spine to

foaming Ionian uprise

beneath flex of land

your shores are drowning

mummified arm Indonesian
sailor skin
boxed in glass and lead

call it James

arm is fine

art: GOLDEN DRAGONS

H O L D   F A S T   fingers

to   FULL RIGGED H.M.S.

ROOSTER AND PIG
can't swim

friends become
ink on the knees
held to chin

TA   NM

storm birds report

bright effluence

their feet

are vanishing

night watchers evolve

hollow bones

young gulls have landed

upon his effigy

fuse wires in his sleep

where he is bound

blue effluvium

Vedic *aum*

of imperishable

syllables whirl

the blood

sea is censer

        approaching shore

               smell of myrrh

                     aspect of mouth   river of

                                     lampreys

pocket knife in robotic hand

James cuts leaves of French pages

in nailed down chair

phosphorescent plankton

plume the night sea

night watcher

with bartered needle

inks the backs of his hands

in Greek

Sources for Chinese Poetry

Clouds Float North: The Complete Poems of Yu Xuanji, Translated by David Young and Jiann I. Lin, Wesleyan University Press/University Press of New England, 1998.

Love and the Turning Year: One Hundred More Poems From the Chinese, Translated by Kenneth Rexroth, New Directions, 1970.

Su Tung-P'o, Translated by Burton Watson, Columbia University Press, 1965.

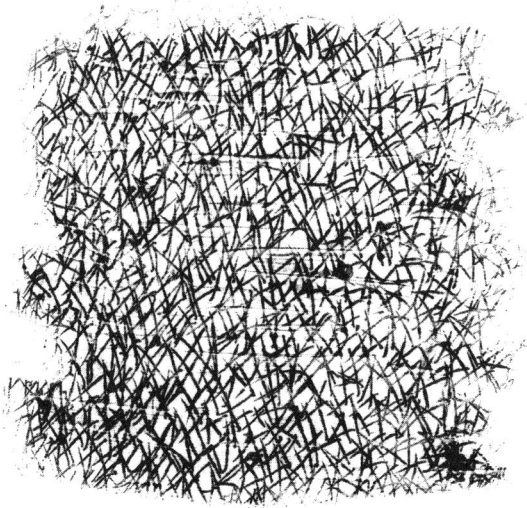

ALSO BY
LITMUS PRESS

For more information visit www.litmuspress.org